THE LAST VOYAGE OF THE LEINSTER
REMEMBERING THE DÚN LAOGHAIRE & HOLYHEAD MAILBOAT

This is the Centenary Book of the Dún Laoghaire to Holyhead Mail Boat - the *RMS Leinster*. It is written in the main by descendants of those who were on the ship when it was sunk with the loss of about 540 lives. These are personal and family stories about the sinking which have been handed down through generations. Our stories arise from the Mail Boat Leinster Centenary Committee's public requests for relatives of those affected to come forward with their own family histories. They have done so on a strictly voluntary basis with proceeds from the book going to fund the centenary and later events remembering the *Leinster*. The focus of this book is not war, maritime affairs or youthful adventure, it is about the human aspects, real people and families from many lands who were devastated by this terrible war-time act in an inglorious war.

Acknowledgements

Published by the Dún Laoghaire Holyhead Mail Boat *Leinster* Centenary Committee/Friends of the *Leinster*.

Printed by: Nicholson & Bass Ltd, Newtownabbey, Co Antrim.

Design by: Gerard Butler, Signal Design & Marketing.

Editorial working committee members: Breasal Ó Caollaí, Niall O'Hagan, Ken Finlay.

Photographic assistance: Richard Cruise.

The front cover features Maude Marsham Rae, rescued by HMS Mallard. Her husband Second Lieutenant Lindsay Marsham Rae was lost.

Any views expressed in these pages are not necessarily those of the committee, the editorial working committee or descendants in general.

Note

Dún Laoghaire (literally, the Fort of Laoghaire) is named after an ancient Irish chieftain, maybe even the fifth century High King, Laoghaire. The 'Dún' or fort - in this case a sea-fort - stood in the area of today's West Pier.

When that location developed as a fishing village it became known as Dunleary, a spelling which to this day prevails on nearby roads.

In 1821, King George IV of England visited the then town council, in a show of loyalty and admiration, renamed the growing town 'Kingstown' in his honour. This remained for one hundred years until the Irish War of Independence was in full swing -but before independence was achieved. The town council decided to respect widespread public demands and local agitations and renamed the town Dún Laoghaire.

To avoid repetition and confusion, this book refers to Dún Laoghaire throughout, except where Kingstown must be used as a title in official documents etc.

Contents

Cllr. Tom Murphy,
An Cathaoirleach of
Dún Laoghaire-Rathdown

Mícheál Mac Donncha,
Ardmhéara
Bhaile Átha Cliath

On behalf of the people of Dún Laoghaire-Rathdown I wish to extend greetings to all descendants of those who were aboard the *RMS Leinster* when she was sunk on 10th October 1918.

The sinking of the *Leinster*, just one month before the end of the First World War, remains the single greatest maritime disaster on the Irish Sea. Over 550 people are thought to have lost their lives when the ship was sunk off the Kish Bank by the German submarine UB-123.

Newspapers at the time were stunned at the loss of life, reflecting no doubt the deep shock in the community. The Irish Times records many families in Dún Laoghaire and Holyhead were touched by the tragedy.

It aptly demonstrates the folly of war, that just nine days later, the crew of UB-123 themselves perished in the North Sea.

It is only in recent years the incident has received wider public attention. I want to commend the volunteers who have organised events and commemorations to raise awareness of this important event in our history.

The loss of over 500 lives in the sinking by a German U-boat of the *RMS Leinster* was an enormous tragedy, robbing so many families of loved ones in such a sudden and violent way. For few but the descendants of those lost, the tragedy later receded into the mists of history, almost forgotten among the great events of the First World War and Ireland's War of Independence.

All losses on all sides in wars leave a legacy of grief and a desire among descendants to remember and to learn more. Ireland's involvement in that futile 1914-1918 war was itself an enormous tragedy; our country was brought into it without consent of the people through a democratic, independent government which was denied to us by the British government. Out of that experience our opposition to military power blocs and imperialist wars was strengthened and the principles of military neutrality and independent foreign policy were established. Those principles remain vital today.

We owe it to all who perished in the sinking of the *Leinster*, and to all casualties of war, to work ever more determinedly for disarmament and for the peaceful settlement of international disputes.

Cuimhnímíd orthu siúd uile a fuair bás agus muid ag obair le chéile ar son na síochána.

Ann Kennedy,
Mayor of Holyhead

H.E. Robin Barnett,
British Ambassador to
Ireland

H.E. Matthias Höpfner,
Ambassador of the
Federal Republic of
Germany to Ireland

The story of the *RMS Leinster* is part of the history of Holyhead and Ireland. The Holyhead Town Council is privileged to be part of this commemorative year.

The memories and stories brought together in this book will ensure that families who lost loved ones will have an album of faces and places as a record of the event that happened one hundred years ago.

The book will also strengthen the friendships that have developed between Wales and Ireland over the years and bring us even closer together.

The commemoration of the sinking of *RMS Leinster* will be yet another significant event in the decade of centenary commemorations.

This series of commemorations, starting in 2012, has offered us who share these islands an opportunity to explore and reflect on key episodes of our past. Over the last five years we have done so in a spirit of historical accuracy, mutual respect, inclusiveness and reconciliation. This has undoubtedly contributed a great deal to the strong and settled relationship that we enjoy between our two countries today.

I would like to commend the Centenary Committee for their significant endeavour to commemorate the sinking of *RMS Leinster*. In particular, I would congratulate the Committee on the production of the Centenary Book which is a worthy contribution to the very positive renaissance in exploring the shared history of our islands.

To the descendants of all those who were embarked on the *Leinster* on that fateful day on 10th October 1918 - whether civilian, medic, postal worker, soldier, sailor or airman - I believe that this book and the events planned for 2018 provide the opportunity to remember our forebears in a respectful and inclusive manner fitting of their personal service during the momentous events of the Great War.

"If the dead could speak, there would be no more war," stated German Nobel Laureate Heinrich Böll, who was born 100 years ago and spent large parts of his life in Ireland. And where the dead can't speak, we shall give them a voice.

That is why I would like to express my sincere gratitude to the Mailboat Leinster Committee for marking this important centenary. One month and one day before the end of the First World War, German submarine 123 sank the *RMS Leinster*, killing 501 people. A week later, submarine 123 hit a mine and the entire crew died as well.

By commemorating these and other victims of the World Wars, we remind ourselves of how precious, and how vulnerable, peace is. Germany has a particular historical responsibility to ensure that the atrocities committed during the World Wars are never forgotten. For us, peace is inextricably linked to the European Union. Only together will we be able to cope with the challenges of the future and to safeguard security, prosperity and peace. In other words, Europe is not only an answer to the past. It is an answer to the future.

The truth was also a casualty

By Breasal Ó Caollaí

The *Leinster* was one of four ships providing the sea connection between Dún Laoghaire and Holyhead in the years leading up to the 1914 - 1918 war. The ships, each named after one of the four Irish provinces, were operated by a privately owned firm - The City of Dublin Steam Packet Company.

The carriage of mail between both countries was its central role with post office employees sorting the mail as the ship travelled. Carrying passengers between both port towns was another important commercial activity, as was the provision of much needed employment, in those days of extensive dire poverty.

During the course of the Great War - as World War 1 was known at the time - the military authorities ordered the company to help the war effort by providing space on each crossing for soldiers. The operator had no alternative but to do so. On occasions, paying-passengers were turned away from sailings because the ship was at maximum capacity. This often caused ugly scenes.

On the morning of Thursday, October 10, 1918, the *Leinster* set sail, from Dún Laoghaire's Carlisle Pier. Aboard were an estimated 77 crew, 22 postal sorters (250 sacks of mail), approximately 180 civilians and in the region of 500 soldiers.

Exact records were not maintained in those days. As a result. a lot of 'information' later presented as 'fact' is in reality estimates or just good guess work. Family stories handed down through generations is arguably a better means of establishing the truth especially as families have no agenda other than remembering their dead.

It is clear that the ship's crew was predominantly Irish and Welsh, while the ordinary paying passengers came from many parts of Ireland, Britain and further afield. The Postal sorters were from the Dublin area and the soldiers came from all over the world, including - Ireland, Wales, England, Scotland, Australia, New Zealand, America and Canada.

Wartime soldiers going on leave were given a ticket to travel to anywhere within "The British Isles". Those with any Irish connections - and some with none - took the opportunity of resting up in war free Ireland.

> More Irish people died on the *Leinster* than on the *Titanic* or *Lusitania*.

Conscription had been introduced in Britain (and existed in Germany) but that was not the case in Ireland. The Irish successfully resisted conscription although the Irish Parliamentary Party leader, John Redmond, had successfully urged many Irishmen to join up. The economic conditions of the time were such that in many cases the only alternative to starvation for many families was for the sons to join the British Army or navy.

Just before 9am the *Leinster* set sail from the Carlisle Pier, Dún Laoghaire. The weather was reasonably good but rough weather was expected during the journey. Between 9.30 and 9.40a.m. the *Leinster* passed the Kish Light (then a vessel). Shortly afterwards the German submarine U-123 spotted the ship and began firing its torpedoes.

Opposite page: *Leinster* survivors, October 10th 1918. Inset: Robert Ramm, captain of the German submarine U-123.

The Governments of Britain and Germany were at war in the interests of retaining and expanding empire. "Britannia" ruled the waves and therefore world trade. The German Imperial Government was determined to expand its commerce and scientific know-how through world trade. The British resisted this expansion. In the resulting world war the Germans declared an exclusion zone in the waters surrounding Britain. They warned that all ships within this area were liable to be sunk. The *Leinster* was armed and indeed live (unfired) shells were found in the wreck in more recent times (See page 40). Following World War 1, the British and American victors accepted that the sinking of the *Leinster* was indeed an act of war by not staging the usual war crime trials over the sinking. Therefore there can be no doubt but that the war lords fully accepted that the Mail Boat *Leinster* was indeed "a legitimate target". This also had grave repercussions regarding compensation for victims' families.

The first torpedo missed but the second struck, near the Postal Sorting Room where 21 of the 22 sorters were killed. The hull was breached and water was roaring through - the vessel was sinking. As the vessel turned in an attempt to escape a third torpedo was fired, delivering the final blow - it was this explosion which caused the majority of fatalities aboard the *Leinster*.

Other ships passed the way but were ordered not to assist for fear of more torpedoes. Survivors struggled to get onto the life-boats or hold onto pieces of wood floating on the water. Rescue boats did not arrive for hours. Heroes emerged including Robert Lee, son of the very successful Irish employer Edward Lee - he publicly supported the case for the 1913 Lockout workers just five years earlier- and Dún Laoghaire's William Maher, a crew member, among others. Maher's heroics would earn him international recognition.

The authorities refused any sworn public inquiry.

The sinking of the *Leinster* proved to be the worst ever disaster on the Irish Sea. There were more Irish people killed on the *Leinster* than on either the *Titanic* in 1912 or the *Lusitania* in 1915. It also had a much bigger effect on the Irish people at the time than any of the many other war disasters affecting some Irish.

Many facts will never be properly established. An official public inquiry was refused. Such an inquiry could have addressed the question of why the ship was not properly protected, who was responsible for that, why postal sorters, the crew and members of the general public were put in harms' way, were the popular rumours true that a few had acted badly taking the attitude of "women and children after me", the use of personal arms aboard the ship, did some corpses have gun-shot wounds, as claimed in print? Why there were no inquests held for many of the dead ... these and legions of other similar challenging stories were circulating throughout Ireland in the weeks and months following the tragedy.

A public inquiry could have thrown light on these and many, many, other disturbing questions which arose following the disaster and became a major source of anguish for many families. The lack of a public inquiry together with the shortage of inquests was regularly highlighted in Sinn Féin's highly successful General Election campaign.

That General Election took place two months following the *Leinster* disaster. But the authorities steadfastly refused any public inquiry. As the war ended just a few weeks later there was no justification for citing wartime censorship as a reason for refusing a public inquiry. The officially stated number of 501 casualties has since been proved to have been an understatement.

The City of Dublin Steam Packet Company went out of business in the early 1920s, with the loss of the *Leinster* cited as a major contributory factor.

NOTICE!

TRAVELLERS intending to embark on the Atlantic voyage are reminded that a state of war exists between Germany and her allies and GreatBritian and her allies; that the zone of war includes the waters adjacent to the British Isles; that, in accordance with formal notice given by the Imperial German Government, vessels flying the flag of Great Britian, or of any of her allies, are liable to destruction in those waters and that travellers sailing in the war zone on ships of Great Britian or her allies do so at their own risk.

IMPERIAL GERMAN EMBASSY,

WASHINGTON, D. C., APRIL 22, 1915.

The German Government's advertisement published in America in 1915 warned; "that travellers sailing in the war zone on ships of Great Britain or her allies do so at their own risk."

Post Office workers flex their muscle

By Paul O'Brien

As the 77 crew members and the 22 Post Office sorters on the *RMS Leinster* set sail on 10 October 1918 it was against the background of dramatic changes in Irish society. It was clear to everyone that Home Rule in one form or another was just a matter of time. Sinn Féin was dominant politically, but the working class and trade union movement played a significant role in the unfolding events, that could have provided other options or outcomes for the new state.

The 21 post office sorters who died that day had been part of a mass movement that had supported the general strike the previous April to protest against the British Government's threat to introduce conscription in Ireland.

The British government insisted that conscription must be extended to Ireland; despite the complete opposition of almost all sections of Irish political opinion. Predictably, Ireland exploded in anger. In April 1918 the Irish Trade Union Congress called a general strike against conscription.

The strike was a success across the country. All factories closed, work ground to a halt in railways, docks, factories, mills, theatres, cinemas, trams, the public service, shipyards, newspapers, shops, munitions factories, even the pubs closed. The determination of the strikers to resist led to the British government to shelve plans for the introduction of conscription to Ireland.

The organised labour movement was the leading light in the campaign. Even the *Irish Times* acknowledged that 'April 23rd will be chiefly remembered as the day on which Irish Labour realised its strength'.

Left Turn

As the war in Europe came to a close there was an increase in working class organisation; trade union membership and militancy increased and this was reflected in demands for higher wages and better living conditions. This shift in working class consciousness took place against a backdrop of revolution at home and abroad, and a sense that a different world would emerge from the chaos that had engulfed Europe over the previous four years.

Labour was flexing its muscles; demanding a place in the new Ireland. Unfortunately, the Labour Party's decision in November 1918 to withdraw all Labour candidates in the forthcoming Westminster elections in order to allow Sinn Féin to stand unopposed sidelined the Labour Party in the momentous events leading up to independence and in the decades to follow.

After independence the postal workers continued to sort the mail; in time the letter-boxes were painted green, but otherwise little had changed for them.

Evening Herald; banned - but not beaten

The *Evening Herald* fell victim of the official censor over the *Leinster*. On the very day of the sinking, the early edition of that paper carried a report that the ship had been attacked. The newspaper was certainly first with that news.

As the report did not have the censor's official permission to print the story, the 'G men' under the command of Inspector Mulvehill, arrived at the paper's Middle Abbey Street, Dublin, premises, where they closed down the paper, seized the newspapers' press and occupied its offices.

Later editions on that day - Stop Press Editions - were banned and the paper remained banned for four more days. It was only when the paper agreed to always obtain official permission before publishing any such sensitive matters in future, and as a 'sweetener', to start a campaign to help the families adversely affected by the disaster, that the ban was lifted.

Ironically, the report published which led to the banning had incorrectly stated that there were no casualties on the *Leinster* - probably the type of misinformation the authorities should have been very happy with.

SATURDAY, OCTOBER 12, 1918.

THE LEINSTER DISASTE

LIVES LOST GIVEN NOW AS 451.

GHASTLY SEA SCENE

FURTHER HARROWING STORIES

SOME VIEWS CONF

The latest official figures connection with the torpedoing Leinster are:—

Lost ... 451   Saved ...

IRISH SEA DISASTER

A DEPENDENT'S FUND OPENED

In addition to the intense and widespread indignation at the barbarous outrage on the "Leinster," there is a feeling of deepest sympathy with the relatives and dependents of the victims. The number of lives lost is of such magnitude as to bring bereavement and distress to hundreds of homes. To make some provision for the numerous sufferers from the disaster is a matter of urgent and pressing necessity, and we are sure the people would welcome the opportunity of being able to translate their feelings of sympathy into practical shape.

FUND OPENED.

We have no doubt that later on a public fund will be opened for the relief of those who have been so tragically deprived of their bread-winners, but as the need for action in the matter is immediate, the Independent Newspapers have decided to open a fund in aid of the sufferers, and to inaugurate it with a contribution of 250 guineas. We are confident that there will be a prompt and generous response from our readers. Subscriptions may be addressed to the "Irish Independent," and plainly marked on the envelope "Relief Fund." They will be acknowledged in our columns from time to time.

The last town they saw...

Dún Laoghaire 1918

By Tom Conlon

The town of Dún Laoghaire was almost 100 years old by 1918. It had developed very rapidly as the harbour was constructed. It was a busy passenger port, an active tourism centre, a shopping destination for the locality and was the administrative, cultural, and social heart of the community of the surrounding area.

Most of the shop frontages along the main streets were quite new and modern; some had been re-faced with red brick at the behest of the landlords Longford and DeVesci over the previous 20 years. Others had been rebuilt from the ground up. Findlaters (now one half of Penneys) had become one of the best grocery retailers in the country and had rebuilt and put its trademark 3-faced clock over the door. McCullagh's next door, (now the other half of Penneys) which described themselves as silk mercers, drapers, hosiers and outfitters, and boot warehouse was newly rebuilt. Another large drapery rebuilt was Morrisons (now Sostrene Grene).

Perhaps the largest retailer in the town was Edward Lee and Co, Drapers (now Dunnes Stores) at 22-24 Upper Georges St.

Ross's Hotel where some of the passengers overnighted before boarding the Mail Boat *Leinster*.

Pictured on opposite page: Scenes from George's Street, Dún Laoghaire circa 1918.

By far the greater number of shops, however were quite small and owner occupied. Many people would remember some of those shop names including Mays Newsagents on the Patrick Street corner, Thomas Brown's tobacconist on the Sussex Street corner, Dixon's newsagents next door, Cooney's pub beside that, Perry's sailmakers and ships chandlers opposite the Carnegie Library, and, of course, Smyth's pub on the corner of Callaghan's Lane.

The Carnegie Library was new, and indeed Library Road itself had just been created. The National Bank (now Bank of Ireland) was an imposing building less than 20 years old, and the Ulster Bank (which has since been rebuilt many times on the same site) was newer. The Royal Bank (now Brian S Nolan's) had added new granite to its red-brick frontage.

The Kingstown Picture House on the corner of Mulgrave Street and Upper George's St was just six years old. Charlie Chaplin, Buster Keaton and Fatty Arbuckle were popular there - they were, of course, silent. Pathé Animated Gazettes (later Pathé News) ran a 4-minute silent newsreel, updated bi-weekly, frequently showing stories of wartime bravery and heroism.

The Pavilion, a massive steel and glass leisure and entertainment centre on Marine Road which had been rebuilt following a 1912 fire, also doubled as a cinema.

Despite constant building and improvements a government report of 1915 reported that there were still over 400 defective houses remaining in the town. The pace of rebuilding slowed to a trickle during the war years.

The tourism business of the town was in full swing and brought visitors from right around the country. The new "swimming and reclining baths" had opened in 1908 on the site of the old Royal Victoria Baths. There was a full range of hotels, and the Royal Marine,

Pictured on opposite page: Hynes & Co. is believed to have been located where Permanent TSB is located today.

Inset: T. Daly's thriving shop on George's Street, Dún Laoghaire, circa 1918.

Top: Murray's shop in Lower George's Street which later became Séan McManus pawnbrokers.

Bottom: Eblana Club members set off on a day's outing from outside the club premises on Eblana Avenue, shortly before the *Leinster* disaster. The Sinn Féin founder, Arthur Griffith is said to be included.

Salthill Hotel, and Ross's Victoria Hotel were considered to be among the best in the country.

The Great War

At a recruitment meeting in August 1915 it was announced that more than 900 men from the town had enlisted, and more were wanted. At the outbreak of the war, the government had requisitioned many of the steamers that plied the Kingstown-Holyhead route, and fitted them either with guns or with hospital equipment. The crews had a stark choice; stay with the vessel and go to war, or lose your job. For passengers, it meant frequent overcrowding on the remaining boats. On January 11th 1918, police had to be called, gangways lifted, and fire hoses deployed to control the crowds on the Carlisle Pier as more than 1,500 were left behind.

Those who could not fight, helped in other ways. A group of volunteers from the town had erected a shed in the harbour to provide refreshments to anyone in uniform. Temporary hospitals to treat the wounded had been set up in a number of places in the area. One such hospital was at Corrig Castle where Corrig Park was later built. Another was on Monkstown Avenue at Monkstown House, now Monkstown Community Centre.

Daily living

A combination of massive price inflation and scarcity of goods in the shops meant that people had to be quite frugal. The war had created a demand for all of the materials of war, but towns like Dún Laoghaire were ill-equipped to take advantage of that demand; the town had no manufacturing industry of significance.

If we look at the prices of the time the initial reaction is that things looked cheap. The Irish Independent newspaper was one penny (less than half a cent). A pint of porter was seven pence in October 1918, more than twice the price it had been at the start of the war four years earlier. Three-bedroom houses in the area were being advertised for around £400, while houses closer to the city were about 30-40% dearer.

Wages were mostly very low, however. Experienced bricklayers or carpenters could get about one shilling and three pence per hour. With a long working week he'd get about £3 per week. The rate for male workers in the shirt-making business was raised in late Summer 1914 to 8 pence per hour for males and to 6 pence for females. The going rate for a live-in domestic servant was about £15 a year.

Events and distractions

In the summertime, there were regular fund-raising events. A Fête was held each July in aid of the Workingmen's Club. One of the unusual events there was a tug-o-war between the various urban councils along the coast – Blackrock, Kingstown, Dalkey and Killiney. A September fete in each of the war years was a fund-raising event in aid of wounded Belgian soldiers. Military bands played at these fetes, but one of the highlights was always the Carriglea Industrial School band.

Through the Summer and Autumn of 1918, life went on as normal. The Dún Laoghaire Fête and Flower Show was held in the People's Park on August 1st, but the organisers complained that competitors paid more attention to size than to quality. Later in August, the People's Park was also the location for a Japanese Carnival. The Dublin Metropolitan Police band played on the East Pier on Wednesdays and Saturdays. The army recruiters were back in town looking for more - this time, they got much heckling from the crowd. The Yacht clubs held their regattas. There was no anticipation of the tragedy that was about to unfold.

A tram outside the Christian Institute on Upper George's Street, Dún Laoghaire, circa 1918.

A general view of the then busy
Dún Laoghaire port.

...and the town they failed to reach

Holyhead 1918

By Dr Gareth Huws

Holyhead has always been considered special by the Irish people – the first landfall as they were forced to emigrate, and the last departure point if ever they returned. In both good times and bad, the journey across the Irish Sea was significant and, as Joyce states in *Ulysses*, there was always a 'Mailboat, near Holyhead by now'. But in 1918, the year of the sinking of the 'S.S. *Leinster*', what sort of place was Holyhead?

The first and last sight passengers on the Mail Boat saw in Holyhead. The Holyhead Hotel was located at the landing stage while pictured on the right the ship connected to the trains for all parts of Wales and England.

In 1918, the population of the town was 10,500, and in that final year of the Great War, four of every five adult males in the town were either on active military service, or working - on the railway, the harbour, or the packet boats running to and from Ireland. (At that time, 12 people in every thousand of the UK population worked for one of the railway companies, whilst in Holyhead, quite significantly, 150 people in every thousand were thus employed). Around 80% of the population were first-language Welsh speakers, and for the most part families lived in terraced housing, many of which were owned by the nearby Penrhos Estate.

4614. HOLYHEAD: HOTEL & LANDING STAGE.

ENGLAND & IRELAND
· VIA HOLYHEAD ·

Main picture: '*Leinster*' sailing from Ireland before onset of war.

Above left: Horse and carriage, Holyhead, 1916-18.

Above right: Small boy in Holyhead's Market Street during 1914-18.

In 1914 a report noted that Holyhead and the County of Anglesey had one of the highest levels of tuberculosis in Britain – a disease associated with poor sanitation and poverty. Food rationing had been introduced in July 1918 and basic foodstuffs such as sugar, butter, margarine, cheese and meat were in short supply. During 1914 the people of the town took to the streets to protest about shopkeepers who had tried to exploit the situation by grossly increasing their prices. At that time, the average wage of railway workers was 21 shillings per week (£1-05p or €1-19) and rent was in the region of 2/3d per week (12p or €0.14). Unemployment was low but so were earnings, and the risk of falling into poverty was always present.

In 1918, Sir R.J. Thomas, a local businessman and philanthropist, donated 50 tons of coal to the poor of Holyhead, and the Penrhos family traditionally distributed coal, clothing and food at Christmas every year.

But poverty was accompanied by tragedy and the 288 names on the Holyhead Cenotaph Memorial bear witness to the terrible toll on the town during the Great War - a toll disproportionate to the size of Holyhead itself. Between 1914 and 1918, Holyhead seafarers were lost not only when the '*Leinster*' sank but also when the '*S.S. Connemara*' went down in Carlingford Lough, when the '*H.M.S. Tara*' (formally the Holyhead packet boat '*Hibernia*' but requisitioned by the Royal Navy) was sunk off the coast of north Africa, and when the '*H.M.H.S. Anglia* struck a mine off Folkestone.

However, the twin horrors of poverty and tragedy failed to extinguish the innate spirit of Holyhead's people. In 1918, the town was lively and brimfull of activities: the 135 members of the Girls' Friendly Society knitted mufflers for soldiers; the four local football teams enjoyed fervent support; the 19 chapels and churches ran a variety of daily social programmes; concerts, plays and

'*Leinster*' at Admiralty Pier Holyhead, 1910.

eisteddfodau (competitions for poetry and music) were held in high esteem; the 20 public houses catered for the town's seafarers (and others!); films shown in the three cinemas were enthusiastically discussed, and the Market Hall and the town's shops attracted a large number of people from outlying rural villages.

The townspeople were open-hearted and generous: injured seafarers and soldiers recieved care in the town's convalescence homes, Mrs Pearson's Sick and Needy Association tended to the poor of the town, the Red Cross held fêtes to raise funds, and even in those difficult financial times, £3,000 was raised in the town to build science laboratories at the university in Bangor.

A community with little material wealth was willing to be more than generous when supporting deserving causes, and its inhabitants were proud to consider themselves worthy neighbours to the people of Dún Laoghaire, Dublin and Greenore.

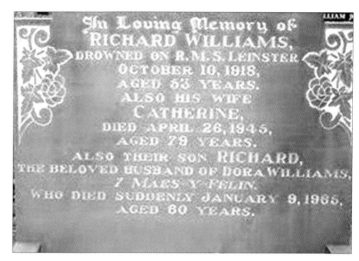

Pictured above: Headstone of Richard Williams who died on the 'Leinster'.

Pictured left: Stanley Sailor's Hospital was founded in 1871 by public subscription, sited at Salt Island, just off Holyhead, Anglesey.

Family reflections

Through the Irish and British media, descendants of those on the *Leinster* when it sank, were invited to put down in their own words, the impact their loss had on their families. These reflections are only a start - there were some 540 deaths in total and hundreds more who 'barely escaped.'

William Maher - Hero of the Leinster Disaster

By his grandson Liam Donovan

William Maher worked as a stoker aboard the *RMS Leinster* and was on the ship when she was attacked and sunk. William, like many other survivors, had to take his chances by entering the cold waters as the ship sank.

A strong swimmer, William managed get himself to an upturned lifeboat and climb on to the side. He had served with the Royal Irish Fusiliers during the Boer War and would have been in some tricky situations before.

The watch presented to William Maher by Dorothy Toppin "as a small token of gratitude for saving her life."

There were others clinging for dear life to the raft, in particular, a young girl named Dorothy Toppin. William held onto this 13 year old girl for two-and-a-half hours before a rescue launch arrived.

As he was helping the girl's mother on to the launch, Dorothy slipped from the side of the raft into the water. Without hesitation William dove repeatedly into the water until she surfaced and he was able to rescue her.

William entered the water a further fifteen times as the launch searched for more survivors.

William was awarded a silver medal and certificate for bravery from the Royal Humane Society in 1919. At the same time, Dorothy Toppin, presented him with a watch in appreciation for saving her life that day.

William was a very strong athletic man, with a large wide moustache that added to the character of the now 'local hero'. Men in Dún Laoghaire still recall when they were young boys and how they all looked up to William and how each wanted to be a hero just like him.

William Maher died on the 11th of June 1953. He was aged 78 and had spent the last remaining years of his life with only one leg, after suffering a serious accident. At the time of his death, William still lived in Dún Laoghaire at 52 Desmond Avenue, along with his wife Elizabeth. The local hero's remains were buried in Dean's Grange Cemetery but, sadly, to this day no headstone marks the spot where he and his wife Elizabeth are buried. The unmarked grave is situated in the centre of the St Nessans section.

Pictures courtesy of Donovan Family/South Dublin Library Service.

Dún Laoghaire County Council in co-operation with the Mail Boat Leinster Centenary Committee are erecting a headstone, as part of the Centenary activities in 2018.

He forgot his sandwiches

By Marie Malone (nee Farrell), great grand-daughter of Adam Smyth

My Grandmother, Mary Clare (Daisy) McCarthy (nee Smyth) was Adam Smyth's eldest child. She was 10 when her father died on the *Leinster*. He was a postal sorter. He left a wife and nine children, ranging in age from two to 17 years old.

Adam was the second eldest of eleven children born to Daniel Smyth and Ellen Magee when the family lived at 19 Sandycove Road, Dún Laoghaire.

Adam had not been rostered to work on 10th October 1918, but received a message that he had been assigned to replace another worker who had taken ill and could not work. The story told in our family is that Mary Clare was the last family member to see Adam as she ran after him to give him sandwiches made by his wife as he left for work.

Adam Smyth is pictured back left.

Ironically, Adam's eldest son, Daniel was a cabin boy on the '*Ulster*' - homeward from Holyhead it passed the *Leinster* near the Kish bank shortly before the *Leinster* was struck.

Adam's body was never recovered and he is remembered on the headstone of the family grave in Deansgrange Cemetery, Upper North Section, Row Y3 119.

A tale of three friends

By Helen Wilson, Omagh, Co. Tyrone

My grandmothers two nephews were Andrew and Alexander Burleigh from near Enniskillen, County Fermanagh. In the 1911 census they were 18 and 15 respectively. Andrew joined the Royal Inniskilling Fusiliers and was very badly injured in WWI.

In a WWI memorial book there is a photo of Andrew and Alexander along with an Australian, Edwin Johnson Carter.

Further research revealed that when Andrew, having been badly injured in battle, was sent to hospital to recuperate he was in the same ward as Carter. Alexander Burleigh went to visit his brother in hospital and was returning home on the *Leinster*, along with Carter, who had just been released from hospital.

It turned out that Carter had two sisters who had Burleigh cousins in Australia. So, not just friends but relatives.

Alexander's body was returned to Enniskillen for burial. Andrew lived to an old age but always had a very bad limp from his injuries.

Fanny Saunders.

Her red shoes stood out

By Darren Blackmore

My great-aunt, Fanny Saunders was on the *Leinster* to visit her daughter in Holyhead, who was gravely ill. Fanny's husband was one of the Lifeboat men who died in the 1895 Dún Laoghaire Christmas Eve tragedy. I remember another great-aunt telling me that as a child she went down to the Dún Laoghaire Pier where the *Leinster* casualties were bring brought ashore.

She could remember Aunt Fanny had bought a new pair of red shoes for her trip abroad, and recalled seeing the same shoes protruding from a blanket covering a body being brought ashore.

Fanny is buried in Deansgrange cemetery with her daughter who died a few days later in October 1918.

Darren Blackmore works with Dún Laoghaire Rathdown County Council.

A New Life and a Sad Death

Edward Moors was born in Birkenhead, the elder of two brothers. His father, John, worked in a local foundry and, when the opportunity rose to work in a similar foundry in Valley, on the outskirts of Holyhead, he and his family moved to Anglesey. It is of interest to note that this Birkenhead foundry was located only three streets away from the mighty Cammel Lairds shipyard - the very yard where the '*RMS Leinster*' was built.)

The family settled in the village of Llanrhuddlad in the north-west of the county. Edward's mother, Elizabeth (Betsan), died in 1889 aged 44 and very soon after the family arrived in Anglesey.

The distraught father felt the need to move away from the scene of his sadness and so arranged that the entire family emigrate to the United States. Edward, now a young man travelled with them to seek this new life. But the United States, with all its promise of new opportunities, was not so attractive to Edward and he returned to Wales.

In 1895 he married Mary, his sweetheart from Llanrhuddlad. By 1901, Edward was working with the LNWR in Holyhead and the family lived at 31 Henry St. in the town. Ten years later he had joined the mercantile marine and when the 1911 Census was taken he was away from home on a sea voyage.

By this time there were eight children to feed and Edward decided to return from foreign travel and join the packet boats sailing between Holyhead and Ireland. He gained employment with the City of Dublin Steam Packet Company and, on that fateful day in October 1918, as the Engineer's Steward on the '*RMS Leinster*' he lost his life. His body was never recovered.

Edward Moors.

From riches to rags

By Carole Hershman, Granddaughter of Arthur Cohen

Arthur Cohen led a life worthy of a novel - climbing from humble beginnings to riches and then dying penniless. His experience on the *RMS Leinster* when it was torpedoed came at a very low point in his life: he was 40 years old and a failed businessman. After his rescue he explored an entirely different area of work and, starting from scratch, rose to the top of his business. This is his story as I have been able to reconstruct it.

His parents emigrated from Tsad, Lithuania (then a part of Russia), to Belfast in 1890, bringing with them their six children. Arthur, aged 12, was the second youngest and the only boy.

In Belfast they established a successful linen business. (How they did this, I can't imagine, because they had been bakers in Tsad).

When Arthur was 15 years old he ran away from home and worked his passage to South Africa, where he hoped to become rich from diamond or gold mining. He did not succeed, but undeterred went to Canada, where he again failed to strike it lucky. So he returned to Belfast where in 1904 he became a naturalised UK citizen.

In 1908 he started his own business, the Donegall Clothing Company. Two years later he was doing well enough to get married. In the following years his wife Louisa gave birth to my mother, Mollie, and a son, Louis.

In 1914, just after the start of WW1, disaster struck. Arthur sent a large shipment of linen from Ireland to England by boat. He evidently thought it unnecessary to insure the cargo against war risks - maybe because at this early stage in the war he did not know about the deadly U-boats. The ship was torpedoed as it crossed the Irish Sea towards Holyhead, and the cargo was lost. Arthur was ruined!

The above story, explaining Arthur's bankruptcy, was the one known to the family. But in researching his story, I came upon another -

Arthur had been running failing linen and clothing businesses in England and Ireland and had been declared bankrupt in both countries in 1915, owing a total of £2,772.

Strangely, not a word was said in the bankruptcy court about the torpedoed goods, leading me to wonder if this story was invented to save face with his family.

He now took any job available, including working for a while as a railway porter.

In 1918, according to my uncle Louis, he made the decision to join the British Army, hoping this would give him a regular income. That was how he came to be aboard the *RMS Leinster* when it began its final, fateful journey from Kingstown to Holyhead.

The ship had been at sea for about an hour only when it was torpedoed by German submarine UB-123. While the passengers and crew were scrambling for lifeboats and rafts, a second torpedo sank the ship. Arthur managed to get aboard a raft after the first hit, but then fell back into the freezing waters - presumably as a result of the second torpedo's violent stirring-up of the sea. He clung desperately to a piece of debris while waiting for help but it was several long and fearful hours before he was rescued.

Grandfather displayed in the hall of his home the framed front page of a newspaper carrying the story. He told me that while he was in the water, though an atheist until then, he had prayed, vowing that if he lived, he would for ever after say the morning prayers required of a Jewish man. His prayer was granted and he kept his promise faithfully.

As a result of his dreadful ordeal Arthur contracted pneumonia and was in hospital for six months. The family was taken in by his wife's sister until he had recovered and was able to work again.

In later life Arthur became a cinema magnate in Britain but died penniless as a result of embezzlement by his housekeeper.

Cabin-boy turned successful businesman

Tom Connolly was a cabin-boy on the ship. His father - known as the Greaser Connolly - also worked on the ship. Both barely survived the ordeal. They lived in Tivoli Terrace, Dún Laoghaire.

In later life Tom set up a supermarket in Dún Laoghaire's Patrick Street. Although modelled on a nearby small shop, the self service concept resulted in Tom Connolly's becoming known as the first supermarket in Dún Laoghaire, if not Ireland.

He was a wise owl when it came to marketing and was one of the first to introduce Green Shield Stamps to promote sales in his supermarket. The stamps became well known nationwide when H Williams supermarket, petrol companies and many others followed his lead by promoting sales through the distribution of Green Shield Stamps.

In the mid 20th century Tom was involved in local affairs and was a long time committee member of the Dún Laoghaire Club (Eblana Club) in Eblana Avenue and his photograph hangs in a place of honour in the club premises to the present day.

Tom Connolly.

Presumed drowned

By Noel French, Trim, Co. Meath

Patrick Faughlin from Trim went missing around the time of the sinking and it was later presumed that he had drowned with the ship.

Patrick was a career soldier, joining in 1908 and serving with the 3rd Batt. Leinster regiment.

He married in 1914 and his youngest son was born in April 1918. When he disappeared in October 1918 after being home in Trim, Co. Meath, on "furlough" (military leave) the military authorities presumed he had died on his way to rejoin his regiment.

In November 1918 his wife wrote to the authorities saying that he "was always in the habit of writing to me regular I am very anxious about him". The authorities could find no evidence of him having been on the *Leinster* but it was the only logical conclusion they could come to.

Mary's letter demonstrated the very real financial devastation caused: "my Separation Allowance has been stopped, myself and my children are in a deplorable state and, as food stuffs are to dear and so scarce, and having no money, I do not know what to do as he left to return to his regiment about the time the *Leinster* was sunk. I fear something must have happened to him."

Bodies in piles on the pier

By Marie Comiskey, Dalkey, Co. Dublin

My uncle Matthew Brophy was one of the post office workers lost on the *Leinster*. He was the eldest son of Walter and Sarah Brophy of Munster Street, Phibsboro, Dublin. There were nine children in the family, and Walter from Kilkenny City, was the chief stone-mason with Fitzpatrick's in Glasnevin Cemetery.

Matthew was 17 years working in the post office and had been married to Molly for seven years. His only child, also Matthew, was born in July 1919.

My father, John, was serving his time as a trainee electrician in the Broadstone and joined the British navy for adventure in 1912. He was home on leave from Madras, India, in October 1918, when word came through of the attack on the *Leinster*.

He was sent to Dún Laoghaire to collect his brother's body as his mother and sister-in-law thought he was used to this sort of thing being away with the navy. He told me the story of seeing all the bodies in piles on the pier in Dún. Laoghaire. Their heads were hanging one to the left, one to the right but he could not locate his brother.

He met Count John McCormick and his wife who were searching for her relatives. He could not find his brother so he arranged for an empty coffin to be buried with his father in Glasnevin Cemetery.

When he was older and ill, it seemed to be on his mind a lot, he wondered if he had done the right thing in telling his mother and sister-in-law that there wasn't a body in the coffin.

My mother loved to go out to Dún Laoghaire with me to see the mail boat off and listen to the band performances on the pier but he never came with us.

The *Leinster* had strong connections to the Internationally acclaimed Irish singer, Count John McCormack. His wife lost relatives on the ship. Following the disaster they adopted a number of children who had been orphaned as a result of the *Leinster* disaster.

GAA lost players on the ship

By Jason McLean

The Davis GAA Club was the postal workers club. Among its players to die were Tom Bolster, aged 15, Peter Paul Daly and Michael Hogan, both aged 21.

Glasthule Mitchels GAA Club suffered the loss of Bernard Murphy Jnr., aged 23, of 1 Adelaide Cottage, Dún Laoghaire. He was son of Margaret (nee Farren) and the late Bernard Snr. The club also suffered the loss of Patrick O'Toole, 22, who lived at 1 Summerhill Avenue, Dún Laoghaire. He was son of James and Catherine (nee Dent).

There were many other GAA players among the victims and survivors - the GAA was growing rapidly in those days including in Dún Laoghaire where the patriot Patrick Moran was actively organising not only his barman and grocery workers trade Union (now MANDATE) but also the GAA.

Patrick Moran.

The loss of a talented musician

By Peter Scott Roberts, Richard Roberts's grandson

Richard Roberts was brought up at 'Siamber Wen' Llandrygarn, (a small rural village in Anglesey), before moving to Holyhead where he took up employment with the Llewelyn Jones Company of Denbigh House. This Company supplied provisions to the packet boats sailing between Holyhead and Ireland. After marrying Catherine Williams of Holyhead in 1900, the couple went on to have seven children.

As he was a musician of no mean ability, he was regularly encouraged to lead the hymn singing by the Rev. Henry David Hughes who was the Minister of Disgwylfa Calvinistic Methodist Chapel. This minister was the father of Mr Cledwyn Hughes M.P. (later Lord Cledwyn of Penrhos), a leading Welsh politician.

Richard Roberts was also the conductor of a children's choir which frequently won accolades and prizes at local eisteddfodau, and it was therefore no surprise that all of his children inherited similar musical abilities. His dark and dangerous work in the stokehold of the 'Leinster' was a far cry from the pure sound of a choir singing in harmony.

At the time of Richard Roberts's death, the family resided at 55 London Road where Catherine's mother kept a shop. Later the family moved further up the same street to 71 London Road.

The fact that the family photograph had only been taken a few months before the sinking of the Leinster, gives it some degree of poignancy. Depicted in the photo are Richard Roberts, his wife Catherine and their six children. At the time when the photograph was taken Catherine was pregnant and the little girl was born after the 'Leinster' sank.

Richard Roberts never saw his new daughter and she grew up never having seen her father.

Richard Roberts and family.

Two to remember

My maiden name was Deirdre Coffey. My father's aunt, Mary Coffey, was the Chief Stewardess on the Leinster. My mother's father was Christopher Hynes from Begnet's Villas in Dalkey, who was a greaser on the ship. Therefore I have two people to remember.

When we were young we always heard how Mary had survived the sinking but it's only in recent years that I began trying to find out my family's history and began looking at anything to do with WW1., in an attempt to find out if either of my parents had family linked to that terrible war.

There are only two of my father's family still living. One is my uncle Frank Coffey, who is still living in Dún Laoghaire. None of my mother's family are still living but I have cousins residing in the area.

Deirdre Galvin (Lucan, Co. Dublin)

The Blakes, Michael Collins and the sword

By Edmond Blake

My grandfather died on the *Leinster*. He was one of the postal sorters. He was Joseph Blake (Senior) who had lived, with his family, in 167 Clonliffe Road, Drumcondra which is located in Dublin's North City, near Croke Park.

He had three sons and five daughters. His son John (Jack) was a Volunteer in the 1916 Rising and died some time later from his wounds. That was two years prior to the *Leinster* disaster. Another unsung hero of the young Republic.!

Another son, Joe Jnr., had also been active in the 1916 Rising. He saw action in Boland's Mills. He was later on IRA active service in the "Tan War" (also described as the Irish War for Independence or "the troubles") before having to emigrate to America, his health broken, as has often been the case with men on the run. He died during 1928 in America.

The third son, James Daniel, became involved in soccer following his father's death on the *Leinster*, thus starting a family tradition in that sport. However in this case it was not just a sport. It was virtually unheard of for nationalist and especially Republican families to have a son playing soccer in those days – unless there were ulterior motives.

Soccer, along with rugby, cricket and hockey, were regarded as "garrison" or "foreign" sports by most Irish nationalists and Republicans. As all four sports had been introduced to Ireland by the British army based here, they were boycotted. It would have been highly unusual for republicans, like my uncles, to be involved in soccer at any level. In fact those playing or involved in our gaelic games of hurling, football, camogie, rounders and handball were banned from being involved in these four sports. The rapidly growing Gaelic

Michael Collins was also a great friend of the family and regularly stayed in the Blake home.

Athletic Association (GAA) banned any of its members from supporting those four "foreign sports" under the real threat of suspension (the Association's Rule 27). This rule remained in place, and enforced, right up to the mid 1970s. Irish international soccer player, John Giles, recently explained that in the 1950s he had felt he was regarded as being "less Irish" than the rest because he played school soccer. It was well known at the time, and generally accepted that the four "garrison sports" in the years following 1916 was patronised by soldiers and all types of "agents of the crown".

James Daniel, is believed by the family to have played soccer at the highest level in Ireland in those pre-Irish Football Association/Football Association of Ireland days. Family history maintains that his brother Joe regularly attended his brother's soccer matches for the purpose of reporting his finding on suspected English agents to IRA leader Piarais Beasley. Identifying likely English spies and agents of all sorts and then following them to establish their identity is believed by us to have been the name of the game.

Of course, as well reported in books and the national media since, IRA chief Michael Collins was also a great friend of the family and

Liam Whelan.

One of the five sisters, my aunt Elizabeth, later married a Mr. Whelan. Their son, Liam Whelan, continued the soccer tradition and became one of the "Busby Babes". He died in the Manchester United Football Club's plane crash in Munich on the 6th February 1958. In more recent years a bridge in Dublin's Cabra was named after Liam and a postal stamp bearing his photograph was issued by An Post.

regularly stayed in the Blake home beside Croke Park. It is believed that he always left early the following morning and never stayed more than one night at a time, like any man on the run.

In later years, after his footballing days, James Daniel moved to Mayo where he worked for Lever brothers. I am his son, born almost 90 years ago.

The five sisters of the Blake family were active members of Cumann na mBán (the ladies IRA) and their exploits are believed in the family to have often been heroic but there is no established records available, as was often the case in those days.

Another of my aunts, Mary, following her Cumann na mBán active service days, married Myles Murphy. Their grandson, born in 1968, is Aidan Murphy better known by his stage name Aidan Gillen. Gillen was his mother's "maiden name" and she was a native of Sligo. Aidan is best known among the younger generation for playing "Little finger" Baelish in "Game of Thrones", CIA agent "Bill Wilson" in "The Dark Knight Rises", as "John Boy" in RTE's "Love/Hate" and "Tommy Carcetti" in the "Wire".

It was not "off the ground" that Aidan "licked" his theatrical leanings. My grandmother, (wife of Joesph Snr. who died on the *Leinster*) was daughter of Captain Fay who had died at sea many years before the

Leinster. This means both her father and husband died at sea. The Fay family was steeped in the theatre, especially during the national revival and the emergence of the Abbey Theatre. The family was involved in the first production of "The Playboy of the Western World" and following that they brought it to English cities where the play was widely acclaimed. The book "The Fays and the Abbey Theatre" tells the story of that part of our family. Of course the Abbey Theatre's central role in 1916 and the national struggle is well documented and was well highlighted during the centenary events of 2016.

In the course of his fighting days, Joe Jnr. Came across the sword described as belonging to the British General Maxwell of 1916 infamy.

The sword was on public display in the Dublin Custom's House when Joe Jnr. "nationalised" it in the name of the Republic.

Eventually the sword found its way to the Mayo branch of the family where it is a treasured family heirloom to the present day.

Aidan Gillen, best known for portraying Petyr "Littlefinger" Baelish in the HBO series Game of Thrones.

Unfortunately the sword's "trimmings" ribbons, holder etc. were sold during the "hungry" 40s but the basic sword remains intact. Before we appreciated the historical significance of the sword, we had used it to root out rats from the corn on the farm. It is now a treasured family heirloom.

Our family is very proud of its history and personally I was especially delighted to represent the family at the big "Gathering" of *Leinster* relatives held in the Eblana Club, Dún Laoghaire in May 2016 and to have been given the opportunity to say a few words on my family's *Leinster* connections.

Buried treasure

Fanny Wookey was the widow of Frederick Wookey, Justice of the Peace and owner of Wookey Linen Mills in Leixlip, County Kildare.

When Frederick died on the 6th July 1918, his wife sold the business (Weston lodge) and decided to return to her birth place and relatives in England.

She choose to travel on the following 10th October and was drowned on the *Leinster*. Her body was recovered and is buried next to her husband in St. Mary's Churchyard in Leixlip.

Frederick and Fanny had three children, one dying in infancy and her eldest, Frederick Maurice Wookey was killed in France in 1915 serving as an offcier in the Royal Irish Regiment.

Their daughter, Frances Norah, died in 1939 and she is buried with her parents in Leixlip.

Frederick W. Wookey was a JP and water flock manufacturer. The mill was the largest employer in the Leixlip area, employing 50 staff. Old clothes and textile clippings were steam sterilised, cut up and though machining converted to flock for unholstery and bedding.

He became notorious by locking out members of the ITGWU in 1913 despite there being no dispute among the workers.

Bernard (benny) Woolfson sold rags and clippings to the mill. He was a Jewish refugee, arriving from Riga, Latvia in 1903 along with members of his family and a family of the same name but not related by blood. All of them had fled the Russian pogroms.

When Fanny Wookey put the mill up for sale, he offered to purchase it by a down payment in gold sovereigns and an agreement to pay the full purchase price over a number of years. Being wartime and little commerce in progress, she was content to settle for the deal.

Bernard and Rebecca Woolfson (Orthodox Jews and new owners of the mill) had seven children – two boys and five daughters. One son,

Reuben, died tragically at a young age. The boy Louis married outside the faith – a Catholic- Mary Theresa Tolan from Synott place, off Dorset Street, Dublin North City.

Louis and Mary (Mollie/Maimie) had 10 children of whom 9 are still living. I, Harry, am the fourth in the family of ten.

> ... he offered to purchase it by a down payment in gold sovereigns ...

The mill was closed down in 1976, and sold off piecemeal.

When my own son, Conor, was about 10 years old, I brought him on a visit to the Maritime Museum in Dún Laoghaire and showed him the replica of the *Leinster* ship.

After relating the story of his Great Grandfather purchasing the mill with a bag of gold sovereigns, his curiosity only extended to whether the bag was still on the wreck and if it was possible to recover them!

Harry Woolfson

Fifth time survivor

My great-grandfather, Michael Joyce, was a passenger and survived the sinking. Surprisingly this was his fifth ship-wreck and he had a colourful life as he was a Member of Parliament from 1900-1918, he was a founder member of Garryowen Rugby Club and President of the Pilots Association having been a pilot on the River Shannon. He died in his bed in his 90th year.

Anne Ó Broin (Co Waterford)

Saved by a telegram

My grandfather's niece Marie Mellett (born 1870) who was a nun and better known as Sr. Henrietta Mellett perished in the tragedy.

She was a member of the Canadian Regiments and Services Division.

My grandfather was scheduled to travel with her but just before he boarded the ship he received a telegram to return home.

Joseph Mellett (Swinford, County Mayo)

A love connection

Evan Rowlands was born in the small coastal village of Newborough, Anglesey in 1868. At the age of only 14 years he left his home and 'went to sea', a career path which was often the only option for young men seeking to broaden their horizons and to escape from rural poverty. He served in the mercantile marine for over 30 years, having enrolled in the Royal Naval Reserve (RNR) in 1897. In 1914, he was employed by the City of Dublin Steam Packet Company as a Quarter Master on their Cross-Channel Ships. When war broke out he immediately left for the RNR and after serving on HMS Caroline he was posted as a Gunner on cargo vessels carrying beef for Dublin Steam Packet Company and, because of his experience, was appointed as Gunner on the 'RMS Leinster'. Ironically, when the war ended Evan Rowlands was denied a Mercantile Marine Medal because he was from Argentina. Such vessels were an essential part of the war effort because the population, both military and civilian, had to be fed and, with Germany attempting a naval blockade of Britain and Ireland, these ships were equipped with a gun as a means of defence.

By sheer good fortune Evan Rowlands survived the sinking of the 'Leinster' and was one of the first crew members to arrive back in Holyhead – probably on 'RMS Ulster' which had passed the 'Leinster' on that fateful morning and had made her return journey that very same day. He was therefore a source of news in Holyhead and people came to his house in 13 Well Street to find out the fate of their family member. One unexpected result of this clamour for news was that Richard Williams, then aged 14, was sent to Well Street to find if there was news of his father, also Richard Williams, who was a Seaman on the 'Leinster'. Sadly, Richard Williams, the father (born in Holyhead in 1865), lost his life on that tragic day and his wife Catherine was left a widow with the care of their only son, Richard, falling on her shoulders. But as young Richard talked to Evan Rowlands about his experiences he met Evan's daughter, Dorothy, then aged 12. In 1939, Richard Williams married Dorothy Rowlands and a new connection was made between two of the 'Leinster's' crew members.

From information provided by Barry and Ann Hillier. Ann is the direct descendant of Evan Rowlands.

A period postcard featuring the Leinster.

I never knew my grandparents

By Anne Dunne

My father's father died when my father, Frederick Dunne, was a 14 year old boy. I didn't know my grandfather's name, until I found my late parents' wedding certificate. Andrew Dunne was my grandfather and when I checked the 1901 and 1911 census, he lived in 2 Adelaide Terrace, Dublin, along with my grandfather's sister, Margaret, and her second husband, James Joseph Godfrey Rathcliffe. They also had two children; Veronica aged 2 and William aged 3 months. I tried to do some research on the Dunne family, but didn't come up with anything.

But I discovered that my great aunt's husband, James Rathcliffe died on the *Leinster* at the age of 33 years. His body was never found and his name is on a memorial in Hollybrook, Southampon, England.

I don't know if there is any more information on James Rathcliffe. I had never heard of the *Leinster* until my uncle, Mick O'Brien, who is very knowledgeable on history, filled me in on the disaster. I found it very sad to think of how my distant relative died tragically and left Margaret with her son and expecting another child. At the time of James Rathcliffe's death the family had moved from Adelaide Terrace to Rehoboth Avenue, South Circular Road, Dublin.

James Rathcliffe's memorial stone in Hollybrook Memorial, Southampton.

...and life goes on...

William Maxwell was a postal sorter who lived in Connaught Street, Phibsboro, which is located close to Dublin City Centre. He had ten children at the time and another on the way. Family stories handed down include that of his wife cooking kippers for a meal on his return from duty. Refusing to believe what was being said about the *Leinster* sinking she continued cooking the kippers.

Information supplied by Marie Sherlock, Granddaughter of William Maxwell

Documents found floating

I am a niece of Nurses Margaret (29) and May O'Grady (24) who were drowned on board.

They were from Mausnarylaan (Mause for short), Newmarket-on-Fergus, Co. Clare.

They were daughters of Francis and Mary J. (nee Kitson) O'Grady and were returning to their nursing duties in England after a holiday at home with their parents.

Mary's body was never recovered while Margaret is buried in the family plot in Quin Abbey. Their original registration certificates were found floating on the water after the tragedy. The certificates are now in my possession.

Mary O'Dea (nee O'Grady) Co. Clare.

Buried four days later

By Martin McGowan (Strabane, Co. Tyrone)

My mother was May Earley who was a sister of Patrick, and married to Charles McGowan from Strabane. Patrick was a serving member of the British Army and was (supposedly) returning to his base somewhere in Wales or England. Fortunately Patrick's remains were recovered and he was buried in our local graveyard in Strabane. Patrick was unmarried, aged 26, and was buried four days after the tragedy.

Saviour of the sea

Compiled by Emily Carraher

James (Jem) Carraher, my father-in-law, was born on the 3rd January 1882 at No. 3 Killmichael, Cahore, Co. Wexford. His back garden, the ocean, Jem left Cahore to join the navy, a tall strong boy of thirteen years he was accepted. And, so began his lifelong journey as a seafarer.

On the 10th October 1918, the *RMS Leinster* sailed out of Dún Laoghaire Harbour on her daily run to Holyhead, a short but perilous journey at that time. Jem Carraher was her *boatswain on that fateful day.

Unaware that a German submarine, 123, one of several, prowling the Irish Sea would soon have the *RMS Leinster* within her sights. On firing three torpedoes, one miss, two would hit the ship, sinking her within eight minutes. Jem, her *bosun, managed to gather several victims, including an infant, onto a raft, staying alongside, as they waited and prayed for rescue. Help eventually arrived and on being brought back to Victoria Wharf as it was known then, Jem faced another scene of horror as bodies lay about, and press and distraught families gathered, seeking news of loved ones.

A traumatised man after the horrors he had witnessed, Jem, with a blanket over his shoulder, walked quietly along the metals to his home in Findlater Street, to the joy and relief of his wife Esther and children.

But the joy would soon be tempered by the loss of workmates, neighbours and friends. This would play heavily on Jem, as the death toll rose and the whole of the community of Dún Laoghaire and beyond mourned.

Jem would go on to survive yet another disaster, as a crew member on the passenger ship, *MV Inishfallon*. While making her way up the River Mersey to Liverpool Port on the 21st December 1940, she hit a mine and sank.

Jem would once more return to the sea and spend the rest of his working life as a mariner. He died on the 7th October 1965, aged 82.

* Boatswain/Bosun is the ship's officer in charge of on deck rigging, anchors, cables etc.

The Eblana Club

Message from Tom Byrne, President, Dún Laoghaire Club (The Eblana Club)

The Dún Laoghaire Club is delighted to facilitate the Mail Boat Leinster Centenary Committee/ Friends of the Leinster for organisation meetings, events, gatherings and in every other way possible. Our club was founded some eight years before the *Leinster* sunk and many of the local victims and survivors were in membership and many others regularly frequented our premises.

Indeed one of my own ancestors, James Hickey, a crew member, of 29 Tivoli Terrace East, was among the victims of the terrible disaster. His body was never recovered. Ar dheis Dé go raibh a hanam dílis. A number of our current members also had family members on the *Leinster*. We all look forward to paying fitting tribute, in the coming Centenary Year, to those who were aboard.

Their spirit lives and can never die

Captain Robert Ernest Lee. Royal Army Medical Corps.

By Michael Lee

At 4.45pm, the early evening of Friday, October the 11th 1918, a traumatised Edward Lee sat down at his desk at his home 'Bellevue' in Blackrock and wrote a desperate and sad letter to his son Tennyson in London. In the letter, Edward tried to explain to his youngest and now possibly second last surviving son, about the tragedy that had occurred to the *Leinster* Mail Boat the previous day off Kingstown and the as yet unknown fate of Tennyson's older brother Ernest.

The family had already lost another son earlier in the war. Both Joe and Tennyson had joined the 6th Munster Fusiliers, of the 10th (Irish) Division at the end of 1914. In August 1915, the 10th (Irish) Division was involved in the landings at Suvla Bay, Gallipoli. Lt. Joseph Bagnall Lee was killed at Suvla Bay, Gallipoli on the 7th August and his younger brother Lt. Alfred Tennyson Lee was wounded on the 9th.

Although aware that the letter with the terrible news about Ernest would not reach Tennyson for a few days, Edward needed to express his feelings to his youngest son. Even today, one hundred years later, this letter makes for tragic reading, its immediacy just a day after the disaster, making it all the more poignant. But it also tells of a father's love for his boys and family.

Captain Robert Ernest Lee. Royal Army Medical Corps.

J.B. Lee and R.E.Lee (circa 1903) Both died in WW1.

Edward Lee and Robert Ernest Lee (circa 1906).

OCT 11TH 1918
Bellevue, Blackrock, Co.Dublin.

My own dear Boy Tennyson,

You will have seen no doubt from the papers the terrible tragedy which occurred to the Mail Boat yesterday. I fear our very dear and loved son Ernest is no more in this world. There is no account of him dead or alive. He left by the boat. The *Leinster* was torpedoed on Thursday morning and she was sunk inside an hour. Oh the horror of it. Your poor mother is bearing up as well as can be expected but God alone knows the sorrow that we feel. I sent you two wires late last night when I could get no tidings at all "that Ernest would not be in London tomorrow," one to Plymouth and one to the Waldorf Hotel, London. I also wired you this morning "Mail Boat Lost Ernest Missing." Of course I don't know If you got them. May the Good Lord pity my boy. You will be very desolate as we are. While I write this (4.45pm Friday) I am expecting possibly a "wire" from them. I fear you will not get this 'til Sunday morning. I am sending you the *Irish Times* of today will "wire" if any good news comes to hand. We fear the worst as we can get no news at all today. Mother and Ted join in unified love to our dear, dear boy.

Your loving and affectionate Father

Edward Lee

Time passed. This letter, along with other family letters, photographs and heirlooms were put away and forgotten for many years. Although the two boys would always be lovingly remembered by the family, the world moved on. The old world that Edward and Annie had inhabited was no more. Eventually, the old couple passed away and the two surviving brothers, Edward and Tennyson found it much too painful to tell their own children the tragic story of their two brothers, Robert Ernest Lee and Joseph Bagnall Lee. It was best forgotten.

As a young boy, I would sometimes take out the two large sepia toned portraits of the two handsome young men in army uniforms and wonder who they were. I was curious to find out anything about them. The pictures were never hung on the wall, but they were kept safely in the house, along with other precious pieces of the past. When I asked my father, also an Edward, about the photographs, he told me that the portraits were of his two uncles who had died in the Great War of 1914 -1918. Joe, had been killed at Gallipoli and Ernest, had drowned when the *Leinster* Mail Boat was sunk off Dún Laoghaire. Then he would go quiet and say no more. Actually, I think he knew very little about his two uncles, because he had been told almost nothing about them himself. Like any child, I accepted what my father said and thought no more about it. Until many years later when I decided to find out what I could, about the two lost boys.

Edward Lee, the father of the four boys, had been born into a Methodist family in Tyrrellspass, Co Westmeath in 1853. The Lees were farmers, but Edward trained as a draper. He moved to Bray in Co Wicklow, around 1878 and in the same year married Annie Shackleton, (born 1859) in Dungar, Co Offaly. The couple set up home at No.2 Goldsmith Terrace in Bray. They had nine children but only four reached adulthood. The surviving children were Edward Shackleton (1879), Robert, known as Ernest (1883), Joseph Bagnall (1888) and Alfred, known as Tennyson (1892). In 1885 Edward and Annie opened their first shop, Edward Lee and Co at their home, No.2 Goldsmith Terrace, where they now lived over the shop. Later that year another shop in Dún Laoghaire was opened, followed by shops in Rathmines and Mary Street in Dublin. The business was a success. Within one generation, Edward Lee who had come from a tenant farm, had transformed his family. The two eldest sons, Edward Shackleton and Robert Ernest, were pupils at Wesley College in Dublin and Joseph Bagnall and Alfred Tennyson boarded at Epworth College in Rhyl, Wales. All four boys would study at Trinity College, Dublin.

In the early 1900's, the family moved to a large house "The Grange" in Stillorgan, Co Dublin. Edward Lee was very aware of his social responsibilities and became interested in local politics in Bray. Voted on to Bray Urban District Council in 1900 and 1903, Edward set about improving the lot of the working people and the poor. As Chairman of the Housing Committee, he was instrumental in the erection of social housing in Bray. In 1908 he was made Chairman of Bray UDC. He was renowned as a model employer, initiating a half day for the staff on Thursdays and a system of profit sharing for all employees.

During the 1913 Dublin Lockout, Edward Lee, although an employer, disagreed with the harsh tactics of William Martin Murphy, owner of the Dublin Tramways Company and the Irish Independent and joined Tom Kettle's Dublin Peace Committee. He was the only employer to do so. The committee tried to find a middle way to end the conflict, but in the end it failed.

Robert Ernest Lee, had studied medicine in Trinity and had graduated in 1910 and gained his M.D. degree in 1911. He was house surgeon to Bootle Hospital in Liverpool for two years. Returning to Dublin in 1912, he was appointed resident medical officer in the Royal Hospital for Incurables in Donnybrook, Dublin. However he decided that he would leave the post after one year. He was then appointed a medical officer on board a cruise ship owned by the Holt Line. When war was declared in August 1914, Robert Ernest Lee joined the Royal Army Medical Corps (R.A.M.C.). He was attached to the 14th Field Ambulance, 5th Division and would spend the next four years in Flanders and France. In May of 1915, at the second battle of Ypres in Flanders, the fight for control of the infamous Hill 60 a few miles south – east of Ypres was a bloody affair. Ernest was involved in bringing stretcher bearers to Blaune - Poort Farm dressing station. The battle was savage and there were many casualties. The scene was recorded by the Methodist Chaplain O.S. Watkins in an article "Captain Ernest Lee. How he won promotion at Hill 60" published in the Freemans Journal on the 10th September 1915.

'Just after dark on the Saturday night, I went out with Lieut. Lee, R.A.M.C., taking a number of motor ambulances with us, our instructions being to try and get in touch with Major Hanafin. Having reached the farm which was to be used as a loading point, we left the motors and proceeded on foot. What a walk! The noise

of the fight, the zip, zip, zip of bullets falling all around us. Twice shells hit the path a few yards in front of us, but did not explode. At last we reached Blaune - Poort Farm, where the Norfolk regiment had a dressing station and where Lt. Brownson, the medical officer was already crowded out with wounded, who were pouring in, in a continual stream. He wanted stretcher bearers. Lt. Lee got on the field telephone and ordered up all that were available. The house rocked with the concussion of bursting shell, bullets beat on the roof, every moment we expected to be swept off the face of the earth. The two medical officers were fine. Both had only recently joined us and were receiving their baptism of fire, but neither gave any sign that conditions were unusual or the danger great. Calmly, with hands that were perfectly steady, they tied up arteries, bandaged shattered limbs and with the dim light of a candle, performed such operations as were needed for the saving of life. All through the night the ghastly stream poured in. I will not attempt to picture that dressing station, blood, horror, shrieks and groans. I wish I could forget myself and do not desire that anybody else should have to carry the burden of that memory.'

Promoted to Captain, Robert Ernest Lee R.A.M.C., would continue to save lives on the Western Front and had boarded the *Leinster* Mail Boat on that fateful morning of the 10th October 1918, to return there.

It was reported that as the *Leinster* was sinking, Ernest helped a fellow officer who had a metal splint in his arm to put on his life jacket and that he had helped a nurse with her life jacket also. It was also reported that Ernest managed to swim to a lifeboat, but when he saw a woman and her child in distress in the water, he jumped back into the sea to help them. He managed to get the woman and child aboard the lifeboat, but then Ernest drifted away. His body was washed ashore off Gorey about a week later and he was buried in the family grave in Deansgrange Cemetery, Co Dublin.

But that was not the end of the story. A while later there was a knock at the door of Bellevue. A lady stood on the doorstep. She was the woman with the child whom Ernest had helped into the lifeboat. She just wanted to call to Edward and Annie to express her gratitude for Ernest's gallantry towards her and her child during the sinking.

My family connection to Robert Lee is through my great grandmother Frances Kaye Belton (nee Bagnall), a niece of Hannah Lee (nee Bagnall) grandmother of Robert.

Hanna Bagnall married Edward Lee 22nd January 1849 in Newtown, Fertullagh, Co. Westmeath. Their son Edward, born 27th March 1853 in Tyrellspass, Co. Westmeath was the father of Robert Ernest Lee.

John H Belton

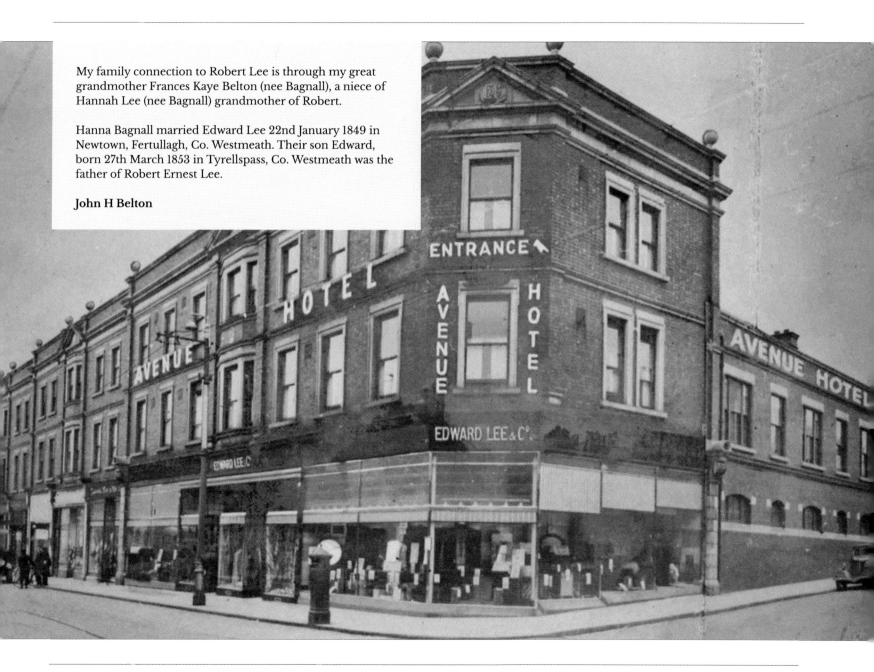

What type of man buys the wreck of a ship?

By Joe Ryan, Irish Coast Guard - Retired

This question is easy if you know it has a valuable cargo.

That was not the case with *RMS Leinster* as she had languished in her watery grave for many years, almost wiped from our memory.

I knew Des Branigan for over twenty years through my association with the Maritime Institute and had the pleasure of visiting him many times during his final eighteen months at Beechfield Manor Nursing Home. I also have a copy of a tape that Joe Varley of the Maritime Institute made when Des told us his life story during a talk in 2001.

Des was born in Dublin, August 26, 1918 into an Ireland in turmoil. He went to sea in the mid 30's and by 1941 found himself a crewmember of the first ship acquired for Irish Shipping, the Irish Poplar. He was an early member of the Maritime Institute who were consulted by the State about Maritime Affairs.

Des did not sit the Primary Certificate but he left school with the three "r's" of reading, writing and arithmetic. He never drank or smoked so on a meagre salary he had a little to spend in port and he had taken an early decision to go on every trade around the world. He turned up at Universities in cities such as Capetown and asked for their help. Lecturers got more pleasure out of corresponding with and helping Des than with their students.

His ship was raided in a U.K. port, probably Bristol, during WWII and he had such an amount of books and correspondence that they concluded that this was no ordinary seaman. Suspecting he was a subversive they confiscated all his material and stored it in a warehouse that was subsequently destroyed.

Des Branigan.

Among other achievements he obtained an MSc in Maritime Archaeology from St. Andrews University in his eighties.

Des ended WWII on British Admiralty tugs. They were deployed to search for stragglers from convoys and carried divers. He learned to dive in the Sibe-Gorman Helmet, complete with rubberised canvas suit and lead boots.

He became one of Ireland's first scuba divers and set about finding and diving on the Spanish Armada vessels on the West coast for which he got a commendation from the Spanish Government.

With likeminded people he approached the State to enact laws to preserve these vessels so that in time all wrecks over 100 years old became State property.

As scuba diving became popular more and more artefacts were being pilfered from vessels, Des bought *RMS Leinster* to stop such plunder, in one case taking a High Court action against a diver. Later, he offered the wreck to the anniversary committee and one of the tasks for the 100th anniversary committee was to find out how we would stand in law if we took it on.

At this stage so close to the 10th October 2018 it is probably best to sit tight and the wreck will become State property on that date.

The Leinster Anthem

From 'Songs of the Wexford Coast', 1948

Des donated one of the anchors to Dún Laoghaire and promised the second one to Holyhead but this may prove more difficult to salvage as it is trapped under the hull in silt.

In an exchange of correspondence with Vice Admiral Mark Mellett, DSO, Chief of Staff of the Irish Defence Forces he said "I think the events around the sinking of *RMS Leinster* were one of the most tragic in our Island's history".

I am sure we can all agree with this sentiment and hope that what has been a local commemoration for the past twenty years will be raised to a National/International event in 2018 in the spirit of detente.

Des's intention was that artefacts from *Leinster* would be housed in a purpose built Museum together with artefacts from other wrecks.

Leinster anchor 2005.

You feeling hearted Christians all in country or in town,
Come listen to my doleful song which I have just penned down.
'Tis all about that German act, that awful tragedy,
When the Dublin Mail Boat *Leinster* was sunk in the Irish Sea.

On the tenth day of October, Nineteen eighteen, the year,
This Mail Boat on her passage went, I mean to let you hear,
With six hundred and ninety passengers and seventy of a crew,
She sailed away from Kingstown Quay and for Holyhead bound to.

In pride and stately grandeur did the *Leinster* plough her way,
And all on board were of good cheer with spirits light and gay;
Not fearing that the U-boat lay hid beneath the wave,
That would send them soon unto their doom, and give a watery grave.

The German monster came on them when they did least expect,
And fired torpedoes at the boat, which quickly took effect.
Her boilers burst; the flames ascend with fury to the sky;
Mid the echo of the deafening dim you could hear the women cry.

Oh, the *Leinster* now is sinking fast; she's going down by the head,
And many, too, while in their bunks are numbered with the dead.
The passengers, their life belts on, unto the boats repair,
While cries for help do rend the skies in sad and wild despair.

Now to conclude and finish - my doleful lines to close;
May the Lord have mercy on their souls and grant them sweet repose.

Beside the Mail Boat, *Leinster*, they quietly now do sleep,
In the cold and changeless waters of the Irish Sea so deep.

A wreck dive like no other

By Michael Schütz, Curragh Sub Aqua Club

On Friday, July 20, 1984, myself and a group of divers from the Curragh, Garda and Army sub aqua diving clubs hired a trawler out of Dún Laoghaire to take us diving on the wreck of the *Leinster*. The wreck lies quite some distance out to sea, beyond the Kish bank, and the dive day was well planned, taking strong tides and possible adverse weather conditions into consideration.

The weather was good and, divided into buddy groups, we managed to get into the water at slack tide to avoid the strong tides in the area. The *Leinster* lies deeply embedded on the sandy bottom at about 30m/100ft.

The visibility was reasonably good, well, you could see about 3-5m. max. by avoiding the sand disturbed by the other divers. There were lots of fish gliding around the structures and over the deck. It was a beautiful sight but also quite eerie.

My dive buddy, Martin Renwick, and I made our way along the railings of the wreck towards the bow, totally in awe at the sight. Suddenly, I noticed a dark opening into a small structure on deck. Nosy as ever, I looked inside the opening and, in the darkness, my torch picked up what looked like the undulation of a rack of wine bottles, all covered in fine sand. I carefully moved inside the small structure and reached out for one of the "bottles". It lifted easily, only disturbing the sand gently as it was totally still inside. I was absolutely astonished to see that it was an artillery shell!!

I passed it out to Martin who looked at me in disbelief. "What is this?" his puzzled face inside his mask seemed to say. I went inside again to retrieve another shell from the rack. There must be dozens on that rack. We found our way back to the shot line and began our ascent up to the surface with our shells under our arms like prize possessions.

There was much interest by everybody on board the trawler in the shells as nobody seemed to be aware that the mail boat *Leinster* had been armed. One of our diving buddies, Com. Frank Donovan, Ret., inspected them. He was particularly concerned about the percussion caps. The cones were corroded but there was a bunch of carbon rods in each shell, twisted like reeds and bound in the middle. One of the jokers in the group pulled a rod out and held it to his cigarette......it lit up like a glow light!! After nearly 70 years at the bottom of the ocean it still sparkled brightly!! The two carbon rods were immediately thrown overboard.

Frank took the shells for further examination to the Curragh Army Barracks and we got them back some time later when they were deemed to be safe. They turned out to be 12 lb British Army artillery shells with their markings still quite discernible.

The *Leinster* – a wreck dive like no other - and one I will never forget!!

Michael Schütz and one of the shells.

Perseverance pays off

William Byrne

William Byrne was still a schoolboy when he began campaigning for something to be done to remember the *Leinster*. His great grandfather, John Donohoe, the chief stoker, was lucky enough to have survived the ordeal. He was the crew member who gave 16 year old cabin-boy Tom Connolly his own safety jacket and happily both survived to tell the tale.

William had been told the story by his grandaunt. At the time the *Leinster* was long forgotten and not even his school history books contained any relevant information. He contacted the Evening Herald and succeeded in having an appeal published for relatives of those who had been aboard the ship to contact him. He also contacted the maritime champion, Des Branigan, the Maritime Museum in Dún Laoghaire and many others resulting in a simple ceremony marking the 80th anniversary in 1998.

In that same year the Holyhead Dún Laoghaire Link was formed out of the celebrations marking the 1500th anniversary of the Árd Rí (High King) Laoghaire having his "Dún" (fort) at Dún Laoghaire.

Over the next few years he convinced Robbie Brennan, Dr. Philip Smyly and others on the Link that remembering the *Leinster* should not only be an appropriate but also a central role of the Link. The Link was established to foster friendly co-operation between Dún Laoghaire and Holyhead on cultural, business, sporting, educational and, indeed, virtually any other activity common to both sides of the Irish sea.

Words to the effect; "See that young red haired fellow, he's always getting onto me about the Mail Boat *Leinster*" was often heard coming from Robbie Brennan and others as they sailed to and fro on

William Byrne.

Link business. Eventually the penny dropped and the Link was instrumental in bringing together the "Friends of the *Leinster*" which successfully organised the first ever community based, with official state representation, event to remember the *Leinster* - that was on October 10, 2003 - the 85th anniversary of the disaster.

The Link in more recent times organised the very well publicised public meeting in Dún Laoghaire during June 2016 at which the current Mail Boat *Leinster* Centenary Committee was formed. Early success of this committee can be measured by the huge attendance at the Relatives Gathering they held in May 2017 and the publication of this book in co-operation with DLR County Council while the Department of An Taoiseach have agreed to become involved in the centenary events.

Meanwhile William Byrne has become a professional musician and sings the *Leinster* Song at *Leinster* events. He is an active member of the Centenary Committee.

The trials and tribulations of bringing up the anchor

Dún Laoghaire man, Noel Brien, was the main mover in recovering the anchor of the *Leinster* which is now on public display overlooking Carisle Pier. His efforts weren't without pitfalls, as he explains here.

I think it was only natural that at some stage in my life I would become interested in the tragedy. Both my father and grandfather spent most of their working lives in the Coal Harbour in Dún Loaghaire as dockers and fishermen. In the latter part of my father's life, he was employed on the Office of Public Works' dredgers.

I too in my teenage years worked at sea for some time. I did a few trips to sea but after a while I arrived at the conclusion that this was not the life for me...as they say in the merchant navy; "He swallowed the anchor." However, I would always maintain a keen interest in all things nautical.

I took up scuba diving in my early twenties as a hobby and after the initial training, I was keen to take a look at some of the shipwrecks in and around Dublin Bay. My first dive on the *Leinster* was in the early 1970s when I and a group of approximately ten divers got together to share the expenses of hiring a trawler. I can remember this first dive turned out to be somewhat disappointing because visibility on the wreck was not good that day and as a result, only a small section of the ship was visable. The most exciting thing for me on this trip, however, was that I was able to take a transit bearing from the land and from then on I knew that I would be able to find the wreck without the use of a trawler's electronics in future.

Shortly before my first dive on the *Leinster*, I had already bought a 26ft lobster fishing boat called Julie Ann, in partnership with two of my friends, Donal O'Neill and Jerry Byrne. It was an inshore craft and not really suitable for the open sea. It was also very slow with a crusing speed of 4-5 knots. A trip to the *Leinster*'s position; approximately 12 miles offshore, would take about four to five hours depending on how

An Ulster University image of the *Leinster* as it lies at the bottom of the Irish sea.

strong the tides were on the day. We only ventured out when the weather was settled and clear so that we could see the land bearing. In fact, some years we didn't take the trouble going out to the wreck because there was too much effort involved.

I remember very clearly my second dive from the Julie Ann. I was with two other divers, Jerry Byrne and Max Neiland. The visibility underwater that day was excellent with brilliant colours emanating from the sea anemones on the wreck as they fed on passing plankton looking a lot like flowers in bloom.

We had decided to explore the length of the sea on both sides. The *Leinster* was 230ft. from bow to stern, which would take up much of our dive time. Our focus at that time was on the ship but when we got to the bottom that plan changed for me. I could see lots of clothing and footwear scattered about in the sand and concluded that it must be from baggage that had broken apart over the years, spilling their contents on to the seabed.

On a later dive, I would realise that this was not in fact the full picture. I was on the lower side of the ship near the bow. There, I noticed a shoe that was partly covered by the sand and I got closer, I could clearly see a trouser leg. Hovering alone, I was able to make out the form of a human being, long forgotten, like so many victims who perished on board the *Leinster*. I was looking at an underwater grave-yard. This sight led me to think that there should be a memorial in Dún Laoghaire Harbour to remember the many lives that were lost in this tragedy and no better memorial than the ship's anchor.

In the mid-eighties I met up with diving companion friends; Brian Whelan, Billy Owens and Kevin Quinn. They were ownership partners of a fast motor cruiser called Shamrock of Gorey. The boat had electronic navigation equipment and this meant that we could locate the wreck of the *Leinster* day or night. At that time, I had written permission from Des Branigan, the legal owner of the wreck, to recover the anchor with a view to creating a memorial in Dún Laoghaire to the victims of the tragedy. The *Leinster* had 2 anchors, the one that I sought was the only one visible on the ship's starboard side. It would have rested on the deck of the ship, bolted into position unlike ships today where they're heaved into a recess in the hull. The bow of the *Leinster* as it sits in the sand has a severe list to port. At some time in the past, the anchor must have broken free and slid

Des Branigan (green jacket), Noel Brien and Brian Whelan at the lifting of the anchor onto Dún Laoghaire Pier. The anchor is now on public display over-looking the Carlisle Pier, from where the Leinster set sail for its final journey.

across the deck over the port side where it was left hanging on the ship's cable in mid-water.

Before we got involved in the project, we wanted to assess whether we'd need to hire equipment to separate this cable from the anchor. I suggested using a hacksaw!!

Everyone thought that I was joking but I wasn't. On my first attempt, I was amazed at the progress I had made. I was almost half way through one side of the link already, with remarkable little physical effort. This was no doubt aided by the surrounding water acting as a lubricant. However, we did have to make three different cuts to the cable before final separation could occur. In hindsight, cutting through the ship's connection to the anchor was the easiest part of the project.

At this point our confidence was high and I let Des Branigan know of our progress. I advised him that we would need a trawler with a good winch to retrieve the anchor. He secured the cooperation of the Commissioners of Irish lights to use their large ship, the Grey Seal when it was working in the vicinity of the bay again. A friend of mine who worked for a lift servicing company, had given me a large coil of wire rope. It was no longer up to the safety standards for use on an elevator but it was certainly suitable for our needs. We arranged to have the wire attached to the anchor in advance of the ship working in

Presenting a programme on the sinking of the *Leinster*. In the studio of Dublin South FM radio station (left to right) Des McCloskey (grandson of *Leinster* casualty James Ratcliffe, Royal Army Medical Corps), Philip Lecane (author) with 1918 aerial photo of the ship and William Byrne (great-grandson of *Leinster* Chief Stoker John Donohoe).

the bay and we left a float attached to our cable on the surface for the ship to pick up.

On the day of lifting we looked on from the Shamrock of Gorey as the wire was taken on board the Grey Seal and the hauling began. When the weight of the anchor came onto the ship she started to list slightly. I knew that the anchor must have fouled in the wreck and very suddenly the wire broke. Our first failure... "better luck next year," we hoped.

Over the next two years, we had two more failures, one with a trawler from Howth which had been organised by Des Branigan. I also got in touch with Finnie McCann who operated leisure cruise trips out of Dún Laoghaire Harbour in a fine sturdy boat called the Ingot. The Ingot had towing capabilities. Finnie, like myself, was a local man and had spent a lot of his younger years down in the Dún Laoghaire Coal Harbour. He was delighted to be involved in the project and contributed his services for free. It was a pity however, that we did not succeed on a further two attempts... the end of another year.

During the winter months, after much to-ing and fro-ing over a few pints, we decided to have one more attempt at recovery. If we were to get a suitable boat again, we would have to find finance because all of our freebies had been exhausted. I decided to go the political route.

Local T.D. Eamon Gilmore was Junior Minister in the Department of the Marine at the time and I had spoken to him before about the *Leinster* tragedy. He agreed it was a worthwhile project and suggested Stena Line as a possible sponsor. He also agreed to get in touch with them on our behalf and subsequently with their backing, we soon had another trawler, the Phoenix Girl skippered by Tommy Creeley on board.

We had lots of time over the winter months in 1990 to plan how we would proceed with the next attempt. At this stage we were very familiar with the area where the anchor was fouling the wreck.

The first thing we needed to do was to pull the anchor shank around by about 45 degrees without lifting it. This would result in the top of the anchor facing a north-easterly direction and, without using the winch, we could drag the anchor free of the wreck with the main engine, with the trawler on that heading.

When the trawler took the strain and increased the power it started to slowly move forward. After about 50 yards we decided to call a halt. We pulled some of the wire cables back on board and decided to send diver Brian Whelan down to inspect the situation. When we came back up he said "all clear, anchor out on the sand, no sign of the wreck". Up went a cheer, success at last! The skipper of the trawler decided it might be too much of an operation to bring the anchor on board. I think it weighed about two and a half tonne. The skipper decided to hang it off the stern and let it aquaplane on our way back to Dún Laoghaire Harbour. On a few occasions as the depth began to decrease, the anchor grounded and brought us to a halt. Each time we took in more slack on the cable and started again. I remember the journey back to Dún Laoghaire Harbour took about 9 hours and we left the anchor on the seabed just outside the Coal Harbour. The Harbour Manager at the time, Tom Vaughan and the Office of Public Works took over the project a few weeks later and dragged the anchor into the Coal Harbour. In November 1991, for the first time in 73 years the anchor was raised to the surface.

Over the next few years the project entailed the cleaning and preservation of the anchor to how it looks today. On the 29th of January 1996 the anchor was unveiled to a large crowd of people including some relatives of the deceased and survivors on the water-front near the Carlisle Pier where the ship used to set sail.

The Leinster remembered in 2003

By Tom Lundon

At around 11.30am in the warm autumn sunshine on Friday morning the 10th October 2003, the casual observer would have noticed an unusually large gathering of people at the entrance to Dún Laoghaire's St. Michael's Church on Marine Road. Scattered throughout the crowd were men and women in the differing uniforms of Police and Military not only from Ireland but the UK, New Zealand, Canada, America along with those of local Firemen, Nurses from St. Michaels hospital, members of the Dún Laoghaire RNLI Life boats, and, of course, Postal Workers. These people along with relatives and descendants had gathered from around the world to mark an event which had occurred on that day 85 years earlier, when the Mail Boat *Leinster* had left Dún Laoghaire harbour bound for Holyhead and was sunk as World War 1 was coming to its conclusion.

However the Ecumenical service which was about to commence to mark the commemoration, was not the first event that had taken place on that day. It had all started earlier that morning, when the naval LÉ Aoife had left Dún Laoghaire Harbour to make its way to the site of where the *Leinster* now lies. In doing so it followed the same course as the *Leinster* had 85 years earlier. Apart from the crew on board, there were members of the Friends of the *Leinster* committee accompanying descendants of those who had been on board the *Leinster*. The Naval vessel arrived on site and was accompanied by the RNLI lifeboat out of Dún Laoghaire the Anna Livia. At exactly 9.50am, the exact time 85 years earlier that the *Leinster* had been torpedoed, wreaths were laid from both the Naval vessel and the lifeboat. Simultaneously four RAF Hawk aircraft from RAF Valley in Wales, did a fly pass over the site. This occurrence in itself was history, as it was to be the first time that the Irish Naval service and the RAF were to jointly take part in a commemoration service.

While the wreath laying ceremony was taking place at sea, the Stena

Philip Lecane, chairperson of the organising committee, delivers a speech on board the LÉ Aoife during the wreath laying ceremony.

The crew on board the RNLI Anna Livia laying their wreath over the *Leinster*.

HSS ship was making one of its then many daily journey towards Dún Laoghaire. On board were the Welsh members of the Friends of the *Leinster* accompanied by a large contingent of people from Holyhead who were making their way to Dún Laoghaire to participate in the ceremony. We were to learn from them on their arrival that during their journey over, the Captain of the Stena had made an announcement to all passengers on board detailing the background to the events and the ceremony that was at that moment taking place at the *Leinster* site. Closing down all entertainment on board, he then asked all to observe two minutes silence which was impeccably observed. At the conclusion of the two minutes and perfectly on cue, the four RAF Hawks which were returning to base did a fly past of the ship. All on board who had worked so hard towards this day, say that it was a very emotional and powerful moment.

As the Holyhead Contingent, arrived in the port, they made their way up to St. Michael's Church where the Ecumenical service was about to commence. On the stroke of midday, two minutes silence was held which was observed around the town and the harbour. At the conclusion of the service, all those who had gathered formed up outside the church, a Colour Party from the local Reserve Defence Forces was forming. The procession then made its way down Marine Road led by the Army No 1 Band marched to Queens Road to the site of the anchor. On arrival at the anchor, speeches were made by Irish and Welsh dignitaries including Albert Owen MP for Anglesey, Jeff Evans, Mayor of Holyhead, Councillor Denis O'Callaghan, a Dún

Laoghaire Rathdown councillor and postal worker and Philip Lecane, the organising committee's chairperson and author of the then just published "*Torpedoed*".

Tom Lundon, is a Great Grandson of James Honan from Limerick who perished on the *Leinster*. Tom was a Garda Inspector in Dún Laoghaire at the time of the 2003 commemoration- later being promoted to the rank of Superintendent before taking early retirement. He now works with an international airline and is a leading member of the Mail Boat *Leinster* Centenary Committee.

Friends of the Leinster committee members 2003

Ireland;
Philip Lecane, William Byrne, Noel Vaughan, John Moore, Breasal Ó Caollaí, Tom Lundon, J.P. Durkan, Cian Long, Pat Houlihan, Tom Franks, Jim Lyons, Rev. Patrick Mangan, Sr. Margaret Mary Ryder, Peadar Ward.

Wales;
John Cave, Eric Anthony, Richard Burnell, Jeff Evans, John Hodgkinson, Stephen Hunt and Alan Price.

The Ecumenical Service that was held in St. Michael's Church, Dún Laoghaire. At 12noon, 2 minutes silence was held throughout the town of Dún Laoghaire.

The Army No.1 Band forming up ahead of the procession to the *Leinster* Anchor on Carlisle Pier.

Above: The Post Office Mail Packet staff and the camouflaged *Leinster* as it was when torpedoed in 1918.

Pictured right: An Post issued this stamp marking the 90th anniversary. Plans for a Centenary stamp are now at an advanced stage.

Mail Boat Leinster Centenary Committee

The Mail Boat Leinster Centenary Committee was established at a very well attended and well pre-publicised public meeting held in the Eblana Club, Dún Laoghaire in June 2016. The following are the committee members;

John Moore *(Chairperson and National Maritime Museum)*,
Breasal Ó Caollaí,
(Hon. Secretary),
Neil O'Hagan *(PRO)*
Richard Cruise *(Treasurer)*
Noel Blake,
William Byrne,
Gerry Clements
(Communications Workers Union),
David Cotter,
Conor Galvin *(Irish Naval Association)*,
Robbie Kearns
(Communications Workers Union),
Anne Keegan,
Peter Kerrigan,
Tom Lundon,
Eimear McAuliffe,
Jason McLean,
Tim Magennis,
Rita O'Brien,
Ger Ryan,
John Shaw,
Nigel Tonge,
Padraig Yeates *(SIPTU)*.

Events of 1918

January

Forcible feeding of Republican prisoners in Mountjoy Prison led to major protests throughout the country.

First reports of the Spanish Flu. One of the deadliest epidemics in history it was notable for proving fatal to previously healthy young adults.

February

"The Tuscania", carrying American troops, torpedoed off the Irish coastline by a German U Boat.

"Representation of the People Act" passed in Westminster gave women the right to vote provided they were over 30, or married and a local government elector. Conscientious objectors to war were barred from voting until 5 years following the end of World War 1.

March

German U-Boat U19 sank the British ship *Calgarian* near Rathlin Island.

The British authorities arrested Ernest Blythe at Skibbereen for failing to remain in Ulster under military's orders.

"Telemachus", part of Ulysses, by James Joyce was published.

Irish Parliamentary Party leader, and staunch supporter of the British war effort, John Redmond, died in London. He was described as "a broken man".

April

Military conscription for Ireland passed in the British House of Commons. A meeting of Sinn Féin, Nationalist Party and the trade unions organised public opposition to conscription.

National General Strike against military conscription. (see Paul O'Brien's article on Page 7).

May

Aldergrove Airport near Belfast opens.

Sir. John French, appointed Lord Lieutenant and head of the British Army based in Ireland.

Huge anti-conscription rally in Dublin.

"Exiles", the James Joyce play, is printed in London.

June

Sinn Féin's founder, Arthur Griffith, won the East Cavan by-election for his party.

Postage stamps increased in price ending the age-long price of 1 penny.

July

Sir. John French, Lord Lieutenant and head of the British Army in Ireland, banned Sinn Féin, the Irish Volunteers (IRA), Cumann na mBán and Conradh na Gaeilge.

The *Carpathia* was torpedoed and destroyed off the East Coast by U-Boat U-55.

Ration books introduced to control distribution of certain essential foods.

August

"Last Songs" by Francis Ledwidge was published following his death on 31 July 1917.

20,000 London policemen go on strike for union recognition and a pay increase.

Welsh composer Philip Heseltine under the pseudonym Peter Warlock completes writing a number of songs while in Ireland.

October

Mail Boat *Leinster* sunk by German U-Boat 123.

November

End of World War 1.

December

Sinn Féin wins 73 out of the 105 Irish seats in the House of Commons and refuses to take their seats. Among the Sinn Féin members elected is the first woman ever elected to the British House of Commons; Countess Markievicz. The nationalist Irish Parliamentary Party is virtually destroyed.

Wexford (Blues & Whites) 1918 Football All-Ireland Champions.

All-Ireland Finals

Due to civil unrest throughout the country both the Hurling and Football All-Ireland finals were not played until January and February 1919 respectively. In hurling the honours went to Limerick who defeated Wexford 9 goals and 5 points to 1 goal and 3 points. In football Wexford beat Tipperary by one point - 5 points to 4 points, completing Wexford's famous four in a row titles. Both matches were played in Croke Park.